EVERYTHING YOU WANTED
TO KNOW ABOUT GROWING UP

New Growth Press, Greensboro, NC 27401
newgrowthpress.com

Cover, Interior Design, and Typesetting: Alecia Sharp

ISBN 9781645076254 (paperback)

Library of Congress Cataloging-in-Publication Data on file

Printed in Colombia

30 29 28 27 26   1 2 3 4 5

HOW TO USE THIS BOOK

Think of this book like a trail map for a big adventure—your adventure of growing up! You don't have to read it all at once (that would be like trying to eat a whole pizza in one bite). Instead, you can

- **Read a little at a time.** Pick the chapters that seem most interesting or helpful right now.
- **Talk it over.** If something's confusing—or just plain weird—ask a parent, grandparent, or another trusted adult (coach, mentor, pastor). They're on your team.
- **Pause and think.** Sometimes you'll see questions or activities. These are little rest stops to help you reflect on what you're learning.
- **Come back again.** Your body won't change all at once. You might read something now and return later when it makes more sense.

One more thing: If any of this feels awkward, that's normal. You don't have to figure out puberty on your own. God is with you, and he's given you people who love you to walk beside you. Take a deep breath, turn the page, and get ready—you're becoming the wonderful young man that God designed you to be!

CONTENTS

1

GOD'S AMAZING DESIGN

YOUR BODY IS A GIFT

Have you ever climbed a tree so high you could see for miles? Or looked up at the night sky and thought, *Whoa . . . God made all of this?* The mountains, the oceans, thunder, lightning, even galaxies—pretty epic, right? But here's something even more jaw-dropping: God made *you.*

That's right, God made *your body* on purpose and with joy. He didn't just make your thoughts or your feelings; he made your muscles, your bones, your voice, and every last hair on your head (yes, even the ones showing up in new places!). The Bible says that when God created people, he formed us from the dust and breathed life into us (Genesis 2:7). Your body isn't just a shell that you live in. It's part of who you are, and God calls it *very good* (Genesis 1:31).

With your body, you might be able to kick a ball, wrestle your brother, eat a giant burger, build a tree fort, and cannon-ball into the pool. You can laugh, sing, high-five, and even feel that tingly chill when something amazing happens. Every part of your body is a gift that shows how brilliant and kind God is.

And get this, Jesus, God's own Son, came into the world in a real human body, just like yours. He had strong legs from walking everywhere. He got hungry and tired. He had friends, a family, and likely some skinned knees. He *knows* what it feels like to grow up.

Because Jesus had a body, we know something huge: Bodies aren't just okay—they're *glorious.*

The Bible says that people are made in God's image (Genesis 1:27). That means you were created to reflect his magnificence. You're not just *a* person. You're *his* person. You belong to him, and he delights in every part of who you are.

Maybe your voice is starting to croak like a frog, or you've noticed your arms are stronger, or new hairs are popping up, and you're like, *Wait, what's that?!* That's normal. Growing up can feel exciting, weird, and even confusing. But don't forget: Every inch of you was made with God's wisdom and love.

JESUS HAD A BODY, JUST LIKE YOU!

Jesus got sweaty, scraped his knees, and even needed sleep. But Jesus never sinned. He used his body to love, by walking miles to help people, lifting the hurting, and giving hugs and hope. He even gave up his body on the cross to rescue yours.

When you belong to Jesus, your whole self—body, soul, and everything in between—is wrapped up in his never-ending love. You are his treasure from head to toe!

GROWING UP IS GOD'S PLAN

Right now, your body is on *mission grow-up*. You might not notice it every day, but big changes are happening. This stage is called puberty, and every guy (and girl) goes through it. It's how God designed you to grow from a boy into a young man.

Some changes are easy to see, like your voice getting deeper, your muscles getting stronger, and your arms suddenly outgrowing your sleeves! But other changes are also happening on the inside. You might start to think differently, feel things more deeply, or notice new questions popping into your brain. That's all part of God's plan.

In this book, we'll explore how your body works, how to take care of it (yes, even your stinky armpits), how to handle big feelings, and how to treat others with respect, even when it's hard. You'll learn what God says about you and what he thinks about all these wild, weird, and wonderful changes.

Here's the best part: You're not growing up by accident. God is shaping you into the man he made you to be—strong in mind, kind in spirit, and full of purpose. And you're never walking alone—Jesus keeps pace with you.

YOUR BODY IS SPECIAL

Take a second and think about all the awesome stuff your body can do. You can use your body in all kinds of amazing ways. You can laugh so hard your stomach hurts, scarf down your favorite snacks, and build epic forts. You can feel the sun on your face, splash in cold water, and hear the crack of a baseball bat hitting a home run.

Pretty amazing, right? That's because your body is an awesome gift from God.

God didn't make you by mistake. He made you—body and soul—on purpose. The Bible says that God created boys and girls in his image (Genesis 1:27). That means your body isn't just something you *have*; it's part of who you *are*. You were made to grow up, enjoy life, care for others, and show the world how great God is.

Your Body Helps You Explore God's Amazing World

God made some wild and wonderful things like towering mountains, thundering waterfalls, roaring lions, and galaxies that sparkle like diamonds. But out of everything he created, you are one of the most amazing.

Why? Because you were made in his image with a mind and body to explore his incredible world.

Your body can likely do all sorts of cool things! Maybe your hands can draw rocket ships, build block castles, and fix wobbly bike wheels. Perhaps your feet can race with your dog, climb a tree, or zoom on a skateboard. Maybe your eyes can spot a rainbow, and your ears can catch the sound of a friend's laugh or a favorite song.

God designed your body to help you move, discover, create, and play. Life is one big adventure, and your body is the gear God gave you for the ride.

Your Body Helps You Show Love

Did you know that your body can be used as a way to love and care for others?

- You can help your younger sibling zip up their coat.
- You can smile or give a thumbs-up to a friend who feels sad.
- You can high-five a friend who made the game-winning shot.
- You can make space at your table or save a seat on the bus.
- You can use your voice to cheer someone up or say, "I'm sorry."
- You can use your strength to carry groceries or hold the door open.

God made you not just for action, but for *connection*. You were created to live in relationships—to love and be loved. You're part of a family, a team, a church, and God's big story.

So whether you're exploring a new trail, making someone laugh, or helping a friend, you're using your body just the way God meant you to. And that's something to smile about.

When you use your body to care for others, you show what God is like. God is helping you grow not just taller or stronger, but kinder, braver, and wiser. And the Bible tells us something really important: God doesn't just look at how tall you are or how cool your haircut is; he looks at your heart (1 Samuel 16:7). That's where real strength begins.

THE STRENGTH OF BEING A BOY

Being a boy isn't about always being the toughest or the loudest. It's about learning to use your strength to serve others. It means growing in *courage* when things are hard, in *gentleness* when someone's hurting, and in *faithfulness* when you make a promise.

You don't have to be the biggest, fastest, or best at everything to matter. You already matter to God. With purpose, he created you and calls you *loved*, *chosen*, and *mine* (Isaiah 43:1–7).

So as your body grows, your voice deepens, and your shoes suddenly don't fit anymore, remember this: God already calls you loved and chosen.

REAL STRENGTH LOOKS LIKE . . .

Saying sorry when you mess up.
Even when it's hard.

Standing up for someone being picked on.

Finishing a chore without being asked.

Asking for help when you don't understand something.

Telling the truth, even if it gets you in trouble.

Including someone who feels left out.

Speaking kind words instead of mean ones.

Praying for someone who's having a hard day.

True strength isn't just in your arms.
Strength serves. Love leads.

THE BIGGEST CHANGE

As your body is growing, you will notice many changes. Your feelings will grow stronger, and your friendships might change. But the most important change isn't about your body at all—it's about your heart.

The Bible says we all need help because everyone has done wrong, and no one lives the way God designed us to. None of us measures up to how good and perfect God is. That's why God sent Jesus. When you trust him, he makes you brand-new on the inside and welcomes you into his forever family. When you belong to God's family, these amazing promises are yours to hold on to:

- **Jesus forgives me as soon as I ask.** (1 John 1:8–9)
- **Jesus is with me.** He promises to stay close, no matter what changes I face. (Matthew 28:20)
- **Jesus is growing me.** Each day he helps me become more like him in kindness, love, and courage. (Ephesians 4:15)

WHILE MANY THINGS ARE CHANGING

As we talk about all the ways your body changes during puberty, it's important to remember that God is also growing your heart. You are his child, part of his family, and his love for you never, ever changes.

That is really good news because some days you might feel strong and excited while on another you might feel awkward, frustrated, or unsure of yourself. Your body is changing. Your thoughts may change. Even your friendships can change. But Jesus does not.

The Bible says, "Jesus Christ is the same yesterday and today and forever" (Hebrews 13:8). That means he is steady when you feel unsteady. He is kind when you are hard on yourself. He is near when you feel alone. He is faithful every single day.

As you grow, you do not have to wonder if Jesus will get tired of you or stop caring about you. He won't. His love is not based on how tall you are, how strong you feel, or whether you had a good day or a bad one. His love is rooted in who he is.

So when puberty feels confusing or uncomfortable, remember this: Jesus is your steady place. He holds on to you through every change, and he will never let you go.

2

YOUR CHANGING BODY

Right now, you're in that in-between zone. You aren't a little kid anymore, but you're not quite a grown-up. Some days you might feel like a superhero, and other days . . . more like a confused spaghetti noodle. That's totally normal. Growing up can feel like a roller coaster—thrilling, weird, exciting, and bumpy all at once. Yet every single part of growing up is part of God's good plan for you.

WHAT IS PUBERTY?

Puberty is the time in life when your body starts to change from a child's body into an adult's body. It's like a road trip your body takes toward becoming a young man. God planned this journey for you, and every twist and turn along the way has a purpose.

He designed your body to grow and change at just the right time. Even when those changes feel strange, exciting, or confusing, you can remember this truth:

> For you created my inmost being; you knit me together in my mother's womb. I praise you because I am fearfully and wonderfully made . . . (Psalm 139:13–14)

So what happens on this road trip?

Your muscles start growing. Your voice starts changing (hello, voice squeaks). You might notice hair showing up in new places, or that your arms suddenly look longer. These changes don't mean something is wrong; they mean you're on the road to manhood, just like God planned.

And just like any good road trip, everyone's route looks a little different. Some boys hit the road early, and others take a little longer to get going. That's totally normal. Whether your journey is fast or slow, smooth or bumpy, you can trust this: God is the one driving. He knows exactly where you're headed, and he's with you every mile.

So buckle up. This road trip is full of growth, surprises, and the kind of changes that lead to something really good. You are growing into the young man that God created you to be.

THE BRAIN: YOUR BODY'S COACH

Believe it or not, puberty starts in your brain, even before you see any changes on the outside! Your brain is like the coach of a sports team. When it's game time, the coach gives signals so that everyone knows what to do. That's what your brain does when it's time for your body to grow.

There's a tiny part of your brain called the hypothalamus (high-puh-THAL-uh-mus). When the time is right, it sends a message to another part of your brain called the pituitary (pi-TOO-i-ter-ee) gland. This gland is only about the size of a pea, but don't let that fool you; it's a powerhouse!

The pituitary gland releases special chemicals called hormones into your blood. These hormones are like messengers racing through your body while shouting, "It's time to grow!" They tell your muscles to get stronger, your bones to grow longer, your skin to change, and your voice to start deepening. Your body's getting ready for the next big stage—becoming a young man.

SO . . . WHEN DOES ALL THIS START?

You might be wondering, *Okay, but when is all this puberty stuff going to happen to me?*

Here's the answer: **It's different for everyone.**

Some boys start noticing changes as early as age 9, and others don't really start changing until 13 or 14. Most guys go through puberty over several years. It is kind of like a long road trip with snack breaks, pit stops, and a few unexpected detours.

Even brothers in the same family can hit puberty at totally different times. So if your friend suddenly shoots up six inches and starts growing a mustache while you still look like a fifth grader—don't panic. You're not behind. You're just on your own timeline. And you're on God's timeline.

YOUR BODY KNOWS WHAT IT'S DOING

Puberty isn't a race—even if your legs start growing like you're training for one. It's more like a building project with God as the architect. He's designing and shaping you with wisdom, care, and perfect timing. He never rushes his masterpiece.

God Has a Plan for Every Weird Change

Let's be real—some parts of puberty are just plain awkward. Your voice cracks in the middle of a sentence. Your armpits start smelling like something crawled in there and gave up. You find one random hair growing out of your knee. Or a pimple shows up out of nowhere. (Why, body? Why?!)

Puberty is your body's way of preparing you for the future. It might feel like a mystery sometimes, but understanding what's going on can help you feel more confident (and maybe even laugh a little along the way). You're growing, you're changing, and God's got you.

You Can Have Confidence as You Grow

Your body is going through a lot of changes. Sometimes that can feel exciting, and at other times, it can feel a little overwhelming. You might wonder, *Is this normal?* or *Why do I feel so different?* The truth is, change can feel uncomfortable, but it doesn't mean something is wrong. In fact, it means God is doing something right. He's growing you—inside and out—into the young man he made you to be.

As you grow, you might feel unsure sometimes about what it means to be a boy. The world says a lot of confusing things about being a boy or a girl, but God is clear and kind. You don't have to like everything people say boys should like. You don't have to love sports or be tough all the time to be a boy! But you *can* trust that God chose your body and who you are with love. If you ever feel mixed-up or unsure, you can always talk to him. He loves to listen and promises to walk with you as you grow. You can also share your feelings with your mom, dad, or another adult you trust. When you tell someone how you feel, it shows you don't have to keep secrets or be ashamed. It helps you stay close to the people who love you most. And remember—**God is with you in every stretch, squeak, and awkward moment. When everything around you feels like it's shifting, God stays the same. He is your confidence, helper, and steady guide.**

GROWING TALLER AND STRONGER

Have you ever tried to put on a shirt and noticed the sleeves suddenly feel too short? That's a sign that your body is growing just like it's supposed to! God designed your body to grow taller and stronger, especially during this time of life. Sometimes your bones grow fast, and you might notice big changes almost overnight or feel your bones aching. It might feel strange at first, but it's all part of becoming the young man God made you to be.

As you grow, you might also gain weight or see your body shape change a little. That's normal too. Your muscles, bones, and even your feet are all adjusting so that you can grow and serve God in new ways.

Understanding these changes can help you feel more confident. God gave you a body that is good, and he wants you to take care of it. That doesn't mean you have to be perfect. It just means doing your best to make wise choices and treat your body well. Every time you grow, it's another reminder that God is at work in you.

SKIN CARE AND ACNE

Your skin does a lot for you. It protects your body and helps you stay healthy. As you grow, you might notice your skin getting a bit oilier or even see some pimples show up. That happens because of those special chemicals in your body called hormones. Those hormones tell your skin to make more oil, which can sometimes clog pores and cause acne.

Taking care of your skin doesn't have to be tricky. Just wash your face gently in the morning and at night, and try not to pick at any pimples. If you use a light lotion and stay clean, your skin will thank you! And remember, even if your skin changes, your worth never does.

God cares way more about what's in your heart than how your skin looks. The Bible says, "People look at the outward appearance, but the Lord looks at the heart" (1 Samuel 16:7). So while you take care of your skin, remember that true value comes from who you are on the inside.

WAIT . . . WHAT'S THAT SMELL?!

Have you ever walked into a room, sniffed the air, and thought, *Whoa! What is that?* only to realize it's *you*? Don't panic! It just means your body is growing, and part of growing up is starting to sweat more. Your sweat glands are waking up and working overtime, thanks to those trusty hormones. The sweat itself doesn't smell, but when it mixes with bacteria on your skin, let's just say it's not exactly *new sneakers*. It's more like the ones you left in your gym bag all week.

This is why showers are your secret weapon. Washing your body with soap (yes, actual soap!) and water helps rinse away sweat and stink. Shampoo takes care of your hair, and brushing your teeth keeps your breath from knocking people over. And let's talk deodorant. It might seem weird to start using it, but it's like giving your armpits a little backup. It helps stop the stink before it starts. Plus, people around you will thank you, especially those with noses.

And here's something important: Be willing to listen when a parent, teacher, or coach gently reminds you to take care of your hygiene. They're not trying to nag you—they're helping you learn how to respect the body God gave you and how to show care for the people around you. Good hygiene isn't just about smelling nice—it's a way of loving others well.

Staying clean isn't just about not being smelly (though that's a bonus). Taking care of your body is one way to show respect for what God has given you. Your body is a gift, and keeping it clean is like saying, "Thanks, God, for making me awesome, even if I smell a little weird right now."

THE "NO MORE STINK!" CHECKLIST

Because superheroes and regular boys need to stay fresh!

Morning Mission: Time to Smell Good and Feel Good

- Did I brush my teeth (without just wetting the toothbrush to fake it)?
- Did I wash my face (yes, water + soap)?
- Did I put on deodorant (a little swipe, not the whole stick)?
- Did I wear clean underwear and socks (not yesterday's "they're still good" pair)?
- Did I check for mystery crumbs in my hair or face?

Evening Power-Up: Time to Recharge

- Did I take a shower or bath today (yes, full-body clean, not just standing under water)?
- Did I use soap on all the key zones (you know what we mean)?
- Did I shampoo my hair if it's dirty or sweaty?
- Did I brush my teeth again (no shortcuts!)?
- Am I wearing something clean for bed—pajamas, a comfy T-shirt, or fresh underwear?

Bonus Boss Level: Time to Be a Laundry Legend

- Did I put my dirty clothes in the laundry basket?
- Did I ask for help if my sheets or pajamas need washing?
- Did I remember to wear something other than that same hoodie again?
- Being clean doesn't mean being fancy—it means being ready to take on the world (or at least the school day)! Taking care of your body shows that you respect God's design and helps you feel great while you grow strong.

HOW MUSCLES GROW

As you grow, your muscles grow too! During puberty, your body starts making more of a hormone called testosterone. This hormone helps your muscles get bigger and stronger—especially when you stay active.

Testosterone starts increasing at different times for different boys, so don't worry if your body seems to be changing faster—or slower—than your friends' bodies. God's timing for your growth is just right.

You might notice your arms or legs feeling firmer or looking more defined. If you notice that your muscles feel a lot better when you use them, that's a sign your muscles are growing! You don't need to lift heavy weights to build muscles right now. Playing outside, climbing, swimming, riding your bike, or playing sports all help your muscles grow in healthy ways.

Fun Fact: Muscles grow while you rest! That's why getting plenty of sleep is so important. Your body uses that time to build and repair your muscles after a busy day.

YOUR CHANGING VOICE

One day, you might notice that your voice sounds a little deeper. Or that it cracks or squeaks when you talk. That can feel surprising or even a little embarrassing, but it's a normal part of growing up! During puberty, your voice box (called the larynx) gets bigger, and your vocal cords grow longer and thicker. This is all because of that special hormone, testosterone. As your body makes more of it, your voice starts to change.

This transition to your new voice usually takes about three to four months. Some boys' voices change earlier, and others later, but everyone gets there in time. So if your voice starts to sound different or make funny noises, it just means your body is doing exactly what God designed it to do!

HELP!

I THINK I'M GETTING BREASTS!

During puberty, your body goes through all kinds of changes. Sometimes one of those changes is a bit of swelling or tenderness under your nipples. It might even look like you're starting to grow small breasts. This is called gynecomastia (guy-nuh-ko-MASS-tee-uh), and it's very common for boys your age.

What's happening is your body is making more hormones—especially testosterone, but also a little bit of estrogen, which both boys and girls have. Sometimes during puberty those hormones get a little off balance for a while, and that can cause temporary breast swelling.

The Good News:

- It usually goes away on its own within a few months to a year.
- It doesn't mean anything is wrong with you.
- It doesn't mean you're becoming a girl. It's just part of how some boys' bodies adjust during puberty.
- You are still growing and developing exactly how God designed you to.

What You Can Do:

- Wear loose shirts if you're feeling self-conscious.
- Avoid poking or pressing on the area (even if it's a little sore).
- Talk to a parent or trusted adult. They'll probably say, "Yep, totally normal!"
- If it's really painful or you're worried, a doctor can check it just to be sure everything's okay.

QUESTION AND ANSWER: WHAT'S NORMAL?

Q: My legs and arms are getting longer, but I feel clumsy. Is that normal?

A: Yes! As your bones grow, your brain and muscles need a little time to catch up. You might trip more often or feel a little awkward for a while. It won't last forever. God designed your body to adjust, and soon you'll feel more balanced again.

Q: I feel like my friends are growing faster than I am. Am I behind?

A: Not at all. Every boy grows at his own pace. Some boys hit growth spurts early, and others catch up later. God's timing is perfect, even if it doesn't match the timing of your friends' growth!

Q: Why do I feel sore sometimes after growing?

A: That's called growing pains. When your bones and muscles grow quickly, it can make your legs or arms feel sore, especially at night. Stretching, staying active, and getting rest can help. If the pain is really strong, talk to a parent.

Q: My feet got huge all of a sudden! What's up with that?

A: That's totally normal. Sometimes your feet grow before the rest of your body catches up. It can make shoes feel tight really fast! Pretty soon, your body will grow to match those bigger feet.

HAIR HERE, HAIR THERE

One day you might look down and think, *Hey! Where did that hair come from?* You might see it under your arms, on your legs, or even around your private parts. Don't worry, you're not turning into a bear! This is just part of how God designed your body to grow into a man. At first, the hair might be soft and light, but over time, it might get thicker and darker.

Later on, you might see little hairs popping up on your upper lip, chin, or cheeks. Yep, that's facial hair starting to grow! You might even get a few "mystery hairs" that show up all alone and make you laugh. It usually starts slow and gets fuller as you get older. You probably won't need to shave anytime soon—but it's fun to imagine, right?

Some guys get chest hair when they're older, but here's the funny thing: Some don't see it until their twenties, and some never grow much at all. That's not weird—it just means that God makes everyone a little different. You don't have to look like a superhero or a lumberjack to be strong and grown-up.

YOUR FIRST SHAVE:

A Step-by-Step Guide

So . . . you've got some fuzz on your face. Now what?

When hair starts to show up on your upper lip, chin, or cheeks, it might be time for your first shave. You don't have to rush. Some boys shave early, and others wait longer. Some use a manual razor, while others choose an electric shaver, which is gentler on the skin.

When you're ready, and if you choose a manual razor, here are some simple steps on how to shave safely and confidently:

1. Ask a grown-up for help. Before you start, talk to a parent or trusted adult. They can show you what to use and maybe even help the first time. (**Bonus**: You'll get great tips!)

2. Wash your face with warm water. This softens your facial hair and makes shaving easier. You can do this after a shower or just splash your face with warm water and use a gentle soap.

3. Apply shaving cream or gel. Use a small amount and rub it over the area you want to shave. It helps the razor glide smoothly and protects your skin.

4. Shave gently (go with the grain). Use a clean razor and shave in the same direction your hair grows—usually down your face.

- Use short, gentle strokes.
- Don't press too hard.
- Rinse the blade often with warm water.

Tip: You don't have to get every little hair. Less is more when you're just starting out.

5. Rinse and pat dry. When you're done, rinse your face with cool water and gently pat dry with a clean towel.

6. Use aftershave lotion (optional). If your skin feels dry or itchy, you can use a gentle, alcohol-free lotion or aftershave made for sensitive skin. Ask your parent what's best for you.

First shave reminders:

- It's okay if you miss a spot—this takes practice!
- Never share razors (they carry germs).
- Change the blade or razor often to avoid cuts.

If you get a small nick, dab it with a tissue. It'll stop bleeding quickly.

You did it! Your first shave is a big step. It's not just about looking neat. It's about learning to take care of your body in a new way. You're growing up, and that's something to be proud of.

SUPERPOWER SLEEP

Imagine your body is like a superhero's headquarters. Every day you go out and battle homework, dodge dodgeballs, and build big ideas. But at night, your headquarters needs to shut down, recharge, and make repairs. That's what sleep does. It's your body's secret power station.

When you sleep, your brain isn't just snoozing; it's sorting through everything you learned during the day, like a librarian putting books on the right shelves. While that's happening, your muscles are repairing, your bones are growing, and your body is recharging. It's like plugging in a game controller overnight so it's ready to go in the morning.

Skipping sleep is like trying to be a superhero with no batteries in your gear. You might still *try* to fly through the day, but you'll feel slower, grumpier, and way less focused. Even your immune system—your body's "security team"—works better when you sleep well.

So if someone says, "Time for bed," they're not being a villain. They're helping you unlock your next level of strength, focus, and growth.

Your mission:

- Aim for 9–12 hours of sleep.
- Stick to a regular bedtime (even heroes need a schedule).
- Wind down before bed. Read, pray, or listen to something calm.
- Power off screens right before bed. Blue light is like kryptonite to sleep!

Remember: Every great hero knows when to rest. God made sleep as part of how your body heals, grows, and gets stronger. So zip up those covers, turn out the lights, and power up for tomorrow's adventures!

CHANGES IN THE GENITAL AREA: WHEN PARTS GROW

Just like your arms and legs grow, so do the parts of your body that are usually kept private. It's one more way your body shows how amazing and carefully made you are. As you grow, you'll probably start to notice some changes in your genitals—your penis and testicles. That might feel a little weird or even surprising, but it's completely normal and how God designed your body to grow. These changes are your body getting ready for the future—when you'll be a grown man, just like God planned.

You might notice your penis growing longer over time. Your testicles might look a little bigger or hang lower too. Even new hair will grow around that area. Again, totally normal! It usually starts out soft and light and gets darker and curlier over time.

Sometimes, your penis might grow at a different speed than your testicles (or the other way around), and things might look a little uneven. That's okay! Bodies don't grow like perfectly timed robots. They grow at their own pace. Think of it like when one of your feet grows faster than the other before your shoes catch up!

Your body is doing exactly what it's supposed to do—even if it looks or feels different for a little while. And remember that there's nothing strange about what you're going through! If you have questions or are unsure, talk with a parent or trusted adult.

What's an Erection?

As your body grows and changes, you might notice that sometimes your penis gets hard. This is called an erection, and it's something all boys and men experience. It happens when blood flows into the penis, making it firm and stand up. It can happen when you feel something—like excitement or nervousness—or sometimes for no reason at all. Really! You could be reading a book or just sitting in class, and suddenly—boom—it happens.

That's normal, even if it feels a little awkward.

Erections are a sign that your body is growing and getting ready for your future. They aren't bad or something to be ashamed of—they're just part of how God made the male body to work.

What If I Get One in Public?

If you get an erection at school or in public, try not to panic. You can try these tips:

- Sit down with your backpack or a book in your lap.
- Pull your shirt down over your pants.
- Shift your body to a more comfortable position.

Take some deep breaths and distract yourself. Think about something else, like your favorite game or what's for dinner. Finding a way to relax is the key. And if someone asks what's wrong, simply say, "I don't feel good, and I don't want to move." This will allow time and distraction to calm your nerves and your body.

Most of the time an erection goes away on its own after a few minutes. And guess what? Other people probably won't even notice unless you draw attention to it. So just . . .

STAY CALM & CARRY ON!

Remember also that you don't need to get upset or angry about your body changing or about getting an erection at an unexpected time. And never try to stop an erection by doing something physical. This can harm or injure your body.

Erections are normal, but treat them like going to the bathroom—with privacy. If you ever have questions or feel worried about it, you can talk to a parent or trusted adult. They'll understand (really—they've been there!).

What's a Wet Dream?

One day you might wake up in the morning and notice that your underwear or pajamas feel wet and sticky, but you didn't pee your bed. What happened? You likely had something called a nocturnal emission, or what most people call a wet dream.

This happens when your body releases sperm while you're sleeping. Sperm come from your testicles. They're tiny cells that are made once your body starts to grow up. God designed sperm to be part of how new life begins.

Nocturnal emissions are something your body does on its own, usually during a dream, and it's a totally normal part of growing up. It doesn't mean you did anything wrong, and you don't need to feel embarrassed or ashamed. It just means your body is working the way God designed it to.

Not every boy has wet dreams, and some boys don't have them until they're older. Others might have them more than once. Everyone is different, and that's okay.

If this happens to you, just change your clothes and sheets if you need to, and move on with your day.

Growing up can be surprising sometimes, but you don't have to figure it all out alone. God is with you, and so are the people who care for you.

How Should I Talk to My Parents About This?

Sometimes growing up brings awkward moments, like waking up with wet pajamas or needing clean underwear unexpectedly. You might feel embarrassed asking your parents for help with laundry. But guess what? They *already know* that kids your age go through changes like this. You're not the first to experience these changes, and you won't be the last!

If you need to wash your clothes or sheets, you could say something simple like, "Hey, I need to do some laundry today," or "Can you show me how to run the washer?" You don't even have to explain the details unless you want to.

If you feel nervous, remind yourself that your parents were kids once too. They had their own awkward moments while growing up, and they love you no matter what. Talking to them—even about the weird stuff—can actually make you feel better and more grown-up.

Bonus: Learning how to do your own laundry is a pretty cool life skill. It's one more way you can take care of the amazing body that God gave you.

TRUE OR FALSE: ALL ABOUT ERECTIONS

True or False: Only grown-ups get erections.

☒ **False!** Boys can get erections even before puberty starts. It's a normal part of how the male body works, and it can happen at any age.

True or False: Erections only happen when you think about something romantic.

☒ **False!** Erections can happen for all kinds of reasons—or no reason at all! You might get one while you're sleeping, bored, or just sitting still. It doesn't always mean anything.

True or False: You should feel embarrassed if you get an erection in public.

☒ **False!** It might feel awkward, but it's not something to be ashamed of. It's a normal body reaction that happens to every boy and man at some point. Staying calm and handling it quietly is the best move.

A GUY'S GUIDE TO PUBERTY: WHAT TO EXPECT

Puberty brings all kinds of changes for guys. It will affect your height, your sweat glands, and your emotions—along with many other parts of your body. Here are some of the changes you can expect:

✓ Getting taller quickly (sometimes your pants feel too short overnight!).

✓ Hands and feet growing first—your body will catch up later.

✓ Voice cracking or getting deeper—yes, those squeaky sounds are normal.

✓ Hair growing under your arms, on your legs, around your genitals, and eventually on your face.

✓ Skin getting oilier—maybe bringing some pimples or acne.

✓ Sweating more and sometimes smelling a little funky (hello, deodorant!).

✓ Muscles getting stronger—especially if you stay active.

✓ Penis and testicles changing size—they may look uneven or grow at different times.

✓ Erections happening randomly—even during class or sleep (totally normal!).

✓ Wet dreams occurring—your body releasing sperm while you sleep.

✓ Feeling awkward or emotional at times—everyone does (even grown-ups!).

GIRLS
EXPERIENCE PUBERTY TOO

Girls go through puberty too, but their changes look different from yours. Just like boys grow taller and stronger, girls do too. Their bodies begin to grow curves, especially in their hips and chest, and they might start wearing bras. These changes are normal and part of how God designed girls to grow into women.

One big change for girls is something called menstruation, or a period. This is when a girl's body starts a monthly cycle to prepare for having children someday. God designed marriage to be the special place where new life begins. When a husband and wife are married, their love can lead to the creation of a baby, and a girl's period is part of how God prepares a woman's body for that possibility. As part of this cycle, the lining of the uterus (a special place inside her body where a baby could grow) builds up and then leaves the body if it's not needed. That's the bleeding, and it comes from the vagina. It usually lasts a few days and happens about once a month. To manage the bleeding, girls use special products like pads or tampons that help keep their clothes clean and help them stay comfortable.

It might sound surprising, but it's a healthy part of growing up. Some girls may feel a little sore, tired, or emotional during their period, and that's normal too.

It's important to remember that girls might feel shy or sensitive about their changes, just like boys sometimes do. That's why we don't talk about things like periods or body changes in public or joke about them. It's not because those things are bad or gross; they're actually part of God's good design. But they're also personal, and being respectful means respecting privacy. So be kind, thoughtful, and never tease someone for what they're going through. God made both boys and girls in wonderful, unique ways, and we can treat each other with understanding and care as we all grow up.

And if your friends start joking or talking about these things in a wrong way—about girls' bodies, or even about things they've seen online—you can choose a different path. You can change the subject, walk away, or simply say, "Hey, let's talk about something else." That's one way to show honor—to treat others the way God says they deserve to be treated, as people made in his image. Real strength isn't joining in; it's standing up for what's good (Romans 12:10).

RESPECTING PRIVACY

Everyone's body is growing and changing and that's a big deal! Some parts of puberty feel exciting, and some feel awkward. That's why it's so important to be kind, not tease others, and keep private things private.

We don't talk about someone else's body, laugh at their changes, or share things that aren't ours to share. "Respect" means honoring others as people made in God's image.

Why Do We Call Private Parts "Private"?

We call private parts "private" because they belong just to you. That's right, those special parts of your body are yours alone. God gave them to you with care, and he wants them to be protected and treated with respect. They're not for sharing, showing, or touching by others. God always wants your body to be protected and treated with respect. One day, when you are grown and married, God has a special plan for how a husband and wife share their bodies.

Think of it this way: Just like you wouldn't want someone peeking in your backpack or reading your journal without asking, your private parts are not for other people to see or touch. They are not embarrassing or bad; they are treasured. They have an important purpose, and God calls them good (Genesis 1:31).

In the Bible, we learn that some parts of our body are more private and need special care (1 Corinthians 12:23–24). That means we cover them, protect them, and honor them. We do this not because they are shameful, but because they are valuable.

No one should talk about, look at, or touch your private parts. Unless it's a safe grown-up like a parent, caregiver, or doctor who is helping you stay healthy, and then only when you say it's okay. And here's something really important: No one should ever ask to take pictures of your private parts, show you pictures of someone else's private parts, or ask you to send pictures with a phone or computer. That's not just wrong, it's also a serious crime. It hurts people and goes against the kind and respectful way that God wants us to treat each other.

If anyone ever tries to break those rules—even if they say it's a game or try to make you promise not to tell—you can say a big, brave **NO**, get away fast, and tell a trusted adult. You are not tattling. You are protecting something God made and loves—*you*!

Please know that if something has already happened that made you feel uncomfortable or confused—even a long time ago—it is not your fault. It is never too late to speak up. God sees you, loves you, and wants you to feel safe and cared for. Telling a trusted adult is one of the bravest and strongest things you can do.

How Can I Tell if a Touch Is Safe or Unsafe?

Your body is a gift from God, made with love and care. It's yours, and it's meant to be treated kindly. And that means you should receive only good and helpful touches, like a hug from someone you love (when you want it), a high-five, a pat on the back, or a hand to hold during prayer. These kinds of touches can help us feel connected, safe, and seen.

But other touches are not okay. If someone touches you in a way that feels icky, scary, confusing, or just off, it's okay to speak up. Even if they say it's a secret or try to make it seem fun. Speak up right away; it's not your fault. God always wants you to be safe.

Your feelings are like little alarm bells God gave you to tell you when something isn't right. You can always talk to a trusted adult, like a parent, teacher, coach, or neighbor who makes you feel safe. To be ready, make a "Safe Grown-Up List" of people you can tell if something feels wrong or confusing.

And here's a truth to tuck into your heart: God never wants you to keep a scary or uncomfortable touch a secret (Ephesians 5:11). You were made to be safe. You were made to be loved. And your voice is strong and important.

HOW TO TALK TO YOUR PARENTS ABOUT BODY CHANGES

(Even if It Feels a Little Weird)

Let's be honest—talking about puberty can feel awkward. But here's something cool: Your parents have been through it too. They know what it's like, and they want to help you, not embarrass you! Here are some easy ways to get the conversation started.

Start with Something Simple

You don't have to give a speech. You can try something like:

- "Can I ask you something about my body?"
- "Is it normal for . . .?"
- "I read something, and I have questions about it."
- "Can we talk about something kinda awkward?" (That lets them know to be extra chill!)

Pick a Good Time

Try bringing it up when things are calm, like:

- During a car ride
- Before bed
- While on a walk
- While you're doing something together, like folding laundry, working in the yard, or cleaning up after a meal

Use Everyday Events as a Lead-In

When you start a conversation with your parents, you can use an everyday event as a lead-in. If you're doing laundry, you could say, "Hey, I had a wet dream. Can I do my own sheets?" Or, after putting on deodorant, you could ask, "Is it okay if I ask about body stuff?"

Feeling Nervous? That's Normal

It's okay to feel shy or unsure when you start a conversation with your parents. Talking about puberty can feel strange at first, but it gets easier. Your parents will probably be proud of you for being brave enough to ask.

Remember:

- You're not weird. Your body is doing what it's supposed to do.
- You're not alone. Every boy goes through these changes.
- You don't have to figure it all out yourself. God gave you parents to help!

Bonus tip: If talking feels too hard, try writing a note, texting a question, or even showing them a section from this book and saying, "This is what I'm wondering about."

GOOD NEWS AS YOU CHANGE

Your body is growing. Your voice is cracking. Your emotions sometimes feel like a roller coaster—up one minute and down the next. Some days you feel confident and strong. Other days you might feel unsure, awkward, or just plain weird. You might even wonder, *Who am I becoming?*

Here's the truth: You're becoming the young man God made you to be. God loves you deeply and his love never changes. That's even more important than your height, your muscles, or the sound of your voice.

The Bible tells us that all people—even those who seem to have it all together—need help. We all go our own way instead of God's way (that's what the Bible calls sin). We turn away from God and try to live life our own way (Isaiah 53:6). We don't love God, and we don't love the people around us. But God didn't leave us stuck. He sent Jesus, his perfect Son, to rescue us. Jesus took the punishment we deserved when he died on the cross. Then he rose again, defeating sin and death forever. Because of Jesus, you can be *forgiven*, *made new*, and *close to God*. Not just someday, but right now.

And here's the best news of all: God doesn't just care about your changing body. He cares about your heart. That's what the

gospel is all about. Jesus came to make you new from the inside out. Even when puberty makes you feel unsure or different, God's love for you stays steady. He sees all of you—every fear, every question, every growing pain—and he loves you completely.

You don't have to pretend to be strong. You don't have to hide when you feel awkward or sad. Because of Jesus, you can always come to God as you are. He listens. He understands. He's not embarrassed by your questions or frustrated with your feelings. He is your Savior, your helper, and your forever friend.

Puberty can make you feel like you're standing on wobbly ground. But the good news about Jesus provides a place for you to stand strong. He's the one who holds you steady. When you trust in him, you are made new on the inside, even while your outside is still growing and changing.

And during all the changes, he promises you this:

He will never leave you (Hebrews 13:5).
He will never stop loving you (Jeremiah 31:3).
He will never stop working in your life (Philippians 1:6).

3

YOUR FEELINGS AND FRIENDSHIPS

BECOMING LIKE JESUS

Remember what we said at the very beginning? Your body isn't the only part of you that's growing—your heart is growing too! Each day, Jesus is shaping you to be more like him. That means

- learning patience when you'd rather snap,
- choosing kindness when it would be easier to be mean, and
- loving others even when it feels hard.

Just like your legs stretch taller and your brain learns new things, your heart is stretching too—becoming full of Jesus's love.

And here's the best part: You don't grow alone. God's Spirit lives in you, helping you every step of the way. When you feel weak, he gives strength. When you do something wrong, he helps you turn back to Jesus. When you're not sure what to do, he guides you.

So as your body changes on the outside, remember that Jesus is also changing you on the inside. You are becoming more and more the man he made you to be.

BECOMING STRONG INSIDE AND OUTSIDE

Your body isn't the only thing growing right now. Your heart, mind, and faith are growing too. Puberty brings physical changes like taller height, deeper voice, and stronger muscles. But becoming the person God made you to be is more than what happens on the outside.

God cares deeply about who you're becoming on the *inside*. That means learning how to handle big emotions, make wise choices, and treat others with kindness and respect. It means knowing how to talk to your parents, how to be honest even when it's hard, and how to turn to God when you feel overwhelmed or unsure.

Just like lifting weights makes your muscles stronger, practicing honesty, patience, and self-control helps strengthen your heart and character. When you grow in these ways, you're becoming the kind of man God designed you to be—strong in body and in spirit (Luke 2:52).

In the next sections, we'll talk about things like managing screen time, setting boundaries, respecting others, and growing closer to God. These are all part of growing up in a way that honors God's amazing design—on the inside and outside.

WHAT'S GOING ON WITH MY FEELINGS?

Have you ever felt totally fine one minute and then *bam*—you're mad, sad, or annoyed, and you're not even sure why? Maybe a friend teases you and it hits harder than usual. Or you're super excited about something . . . then, five minutes later, you want everyone to leave you alone. What's going on?

A lot of this has to do with puberty. As your body grows, your *brain* is changing too. It's working with new hormones that can make emotions feel bigger and stronger than before. Something small—like losing a game or getting interrupted—might suddenly feel like a big deal. But guess what? That doesn't mean you're broken or weird. It means your brain is learning and adjusting. You're growing.

And here's something amazing: Even Jesus had feelings. He cried when his friend died. He flipped tables when people were being hurt. He celebrated at parties and felt deep compassion for others. Emotions aren't bad; they're a gift from God. They help you understand what's going on in your heart. But here's the key: Feelings were never meant to boss you around.

Philippians chapter four says that when we bring our emotions to God, he gives us peace—peace that guards our hearts and minds, even on the hardest days (vv. 6–7).

Emotions Are Like Waves

Think of your feelings like waves in the ocean. Some days are calm. Other days feel like a storm is rolling through your chest. But no matter how wild the waves get, the ocean floor underneath stays steady and unmoved. The ocean floor is like God—strong, steady, and unshakable. Even when your emotions rise and fall, his love for you never changes.

Sometimes people think that boys shouldn't have strong feelings. But that's just not true. Boys have big emotions too. And during puberty, those feelings might show up in new ways. You might feel grumpy for no reason. You might cry when you didn't expect to. That's normal. It's part of growing. Knowing this helps you give yourself (and others) a little grace. Everyone's figuring this out.

Why Do I Feel This Way?

Sometimes feelings show up fast, like getting really mad during a game or nervous before a test. You might not always know why you feel what you feel. But here's something cool: Feelings are like signals. They help you notice what you care about.

If you feel angry when someone is mean to your friend, that anger is showing you care about *fairness*. You care about *your friend*.

If you feel nervous before a school play, that nervousness is saying you care about *doing well*. You care about *being prepared.*

God made your feelings to help you know your heart better. And when you know your heart better, you can bring it all to him because he already knows and cares. Sometimes feelings lead you toward something good—like caring for a friend who's having a hard day or preparing for something important. But other times, feelings can pull you the wrong way. Maybe you feel angry because your brother messed up your stuff, or jealous because someone else got the attention you wanted. In that moment, you're standing at a fork in the road. Will you follow your feelings, or will you pause and choose what honors God?

Remember: Feelings aren't the boss of you! They don't get to decide what you do or say. God's Word is the light that guides your steps (Psalm 119:105). Even when your emotions feel strong, you can pause, listen to what they are saying, and then choose to follow what God says is right.

The Bible says, "Pour out your heart before him; God is a refuge for us" (Psalm 62:8 ESV).

Next time you feel something big, try asking yourself: *What matters most to me in this moment?*
Then tell Jesus. He listens. Every time.

What Can You Do with All These FEELINGS?

When your emotions feel big—like a roller coaster with surprise loops—you don't have to be stuck. Here are some ways to ride the ups and downs while staying grounded in God's love:

- **Talk to God.** You can say anything to him. Whether you're angry, sad, confused, or thankful, he listens.
- **Write it out.** Grab a notebook and dump your thoughts on the page. No one else has to see it. It helps you figure out what's really going on.
- **Move your body.** Play outside, ride your bike, shoot hoops, or take a walk. Physical movement helps your brain feel better too.
- **Check your heart.** Do you need to ask God or anyone else for forgiveness?
- **Make something.** Draw, build something, play music, bake, or craft. Being creative is a great way to process emotions.
- **Read God's truth.** The Bible is full of reminders that you are loved, known, and never alone. Start with Psalm 139 or Philippians 4:6–7.
- **Talk to someone you trust.** Your parents, a teacher, or a mentor can help when you don't know what to do with what you're feeling.

REMEMBER TO SLEEP AND MOVE

Ever notice how hard everything feels when you're tired? That's not just in your head. Your body and emotions work better when you've had enough rest. So if you're feeling off, ask yourself, *Did I get enough sleep last night?* A good night's sleep is like a reset button for your brain.

God made your body to need rest. He even built a whole day of rest into every week on Sundays! Sleep helps you feel more peaceful and patient.

And guess what else helps? Exercise.

When you move your body—whether by playing sports, biking, climbing, or even just stretching—you're actually helping your brain and heart feel better. So if you're feeling moody or stuck, try asking yourself, *Have I moved today?* It really can help you feel calmer and clearer.

GOD IS WITH YOU IN THE MESSY MOMENTS

Puberty brings big changes to your body, and emotions. Some days will feel awesome. Some days will feel weird. And some days will just feel . . . off. But during all of it, God wants to hear from you. He's not surprised by your emotions. He's not disappointed when you feel overwhelmed. He knows what's happening in your heart, and he cares. God is steady when your feelings aren't. He made you, he sees you, and he'll walk with you through every high and low. Just like the Shepherd in Psalm 23 who leads his sheep beside quiet waters and restores their souls. When life feels stormy or confusing, you can remember: "The Lord is my shepherd, I lack nothing" (Psalm 23:1).

ANCHOR YOUR HEART IN TRUTH

Sometimes big emotions bring big thoughts like these:

- *I'm the worst.*
- *Nobody likes me.*
- *I'll never be good at this.*

Those thoughts can hit you out of nowhere, and they can feel really strong. When feelings are heavy and your mind starts going in the wrong direction, stop and remind yourself of God's truths:

- "I am fearfully and wonderfully made . . ." (Psalm 139:14 ESV)
- Nothing can separate me from God's love. (Romans 8:38–39, author's paraphrase)
- When I sin or mess up, God promises to forgive me because of Jesus. (1 John 1:9)
- God has a plan for my life. (Jeremiah 29:11, author's paraphrase)

You might not feel these things in the moment, but they're always true. Emotions come and go, but God's love stays the same. When everything feels loud or confusing, remember that God is your anchor. He holds you steady when your thoughts are spinning. He's strong, unshakable, and always right there with you.

QUESTION AND ANSWER: FEELINGS

Q: Why are little things bothering me so much?

A: Great question. Maybe someone laughs at your mistake, and it feels way worse than it should. Or your brother takes your stuff, and suddenly you're *boiling mad.* Or maybe your friend forgot something you said, and it just makes your chest hurt.

Think of your emotions like a volume knob. Right now, everything's turned up a little louder than usual. A problem that used to feel like a "2" might suddenly feel like a "9." That's because your brain is learning to handle feelings in new ways.

The good news? This intense phase won't last forever. Your feelings can feel extra strong right now because lots of things are growing and changing—your brain and the hormones in your body, the things you want or worry about in your heart, and even what's going on with friends or at home. All of that together can make emotions feel really big, but with God's help and some time, you'll learn how to handle them.

WHEN LITTLE THINGS FEEL BIG . . .

When something small feels really big, try asking yourself these questions:

- *What matters most to me in this moment?*
- *Have I eaten? Slept? Moved my body today?*
- *What does God say is true about me, no matter how I feel?*

When something small feels really big, try these actions:

- **Pause**. Take a deep breath and slowly count to five. Give your brain a second to cool down.
- **Say what's true.** Even if you feel angry or upset, remind yourself: *This is just a feeling. It won't last forever. God still loves me.*
- **Move around.** Go outside, run, stretch, or toss a ball—moving your body helps calm your mind.
- **Talk to someone.** A parent, coach, or mentor can help you think clearly when emotions are fogging things up.
- **Pray honestly.** Say something like, "God, I feel angry and overwhelmed. Help me calm down and remember what's true."

You are not weak for having strong feelings, but you need to learn to express them in a godly way. God is there to help you sort it all out—every feeling, every moment, and every hard day.

TOP 10 THINGS

EVERY GUY GOING THROUGH PUBERTY SHOULD KNOW

1. You're like a house God is building—one brick, one beam at a time.
2. Confidence isn't about muscles. It's about how you treat others.
3. Feeling confused doesn't mean you have to figure it out on your own.
4. Talk to someone. (Seriously. It helps.)
5. Your body is doing its job—even if it's awkward.
6. Girls are changing too. You're not the only one.
7. God is not weirded out by your body.
8. Real strength includes kindness.
9. Surprises like voice cracks or sudden changes happen—but God is never surprised.
10. You've got this—even when you don't feel like it.

CONFIDENCE IN CHRIST

Jesus didn't just come to teach us how to live; he came to *save us.* That means even when we mess up, feel unsure, or start believing lies like "No one likes me," Jesus still loves us, forgives us, and makes us new on the inside.

God showed his great love by sending Jesus to die for our sins. When we trust in him, we are forgiven, joined to Jesus, and welcomed into God's forever family. That means who we are isn't decided by how we look, what we do, or what others think—it's decided by one amazing truth: We belong to Jesus (Galatians 4:4–7).

Because we belong to Jesus, we are safe, seen, and secure. No matter what happens. He calls us his beloved, his treasure, his own. When the world tells us we have to earn our worth or prove we matter, Jesus gently reminds us, "You already matter. You're mine." Belonging to him means we don't have to figure everything out on our own. He is with us—guiding us, forgiving us, and cheering us on as we grow.

LIKING THE BODY GOD GAVE YOU

Your body is changing, and let's be honest, that can feel odd sometimes. Even your face looks different in the mirror. But every part of you was designed by God on purpose and with love—even the parts that feel awkward or unfamiliar! The way you grow, look, and change is part of God's good design.

You might feel unsure or awkward about how you look. That's normal! But your value isn't based on what's on the outside—your height, muscles, or how fast your voice gets deeper. Your worth comes from being God's masterpiece (Ephesians 2:10).

GETTING STUCK IN THE COMPARISON GAME

It's easy to look at other guys and think, *He's taller,* or *He's better at sports,* or *Why don't I look like that?* Maybe you feel behind, or like something's wrong with you. But that kind of thinking steals your joy.

The Bible says, "I praise you because I am fearfully and wonderfully made . . ." (Psalm 139:14). God made you with care. You don't need to be like someone else; you need to be who God designed you to be. When you're tempted to compare, ask yourself, *Does this help me or hurt me?* And then focus on what really matters: God's thoughts toward you.

SPEAKING THE TRUTH TO YOURSELF AND OTHERS

How you talk to yourself matters. If you mess up or feel awkward, do you say, "I'm so dumb," or "I'll never get this right"? Would you say that to a friend? No way! So don't say it to yourself either.

Instead, say things that line up with what God says, like:

- "God is with me."
- "I'm still learning, and that's okay."
- "This is hard, but I can grow through it."
- "God doesn't expect me to be perfect. He's helping me every day."

The Bible tells us in Philippians 4:8 to think about what is true, lovely, and good. That means even the way we talk to ourselves matters! Instead of saying mean or discouraging things inside your head, you can remind your heart of God's truth. Encouraging words are like sunshine for your heart—so use them often!

YOU'RE NOT ALONE

Growing up comes with big feelings. Some days are exciting, and some days bring feelings that are all over the place. You might feel angry, left out, embarrassed, or just totally off. But here's the good news: Jesus understands. He cares about every part of your life—even the stuff you don't know how to talk about.

You can talk to Jesus anytime—about anything. He listens when you're feeling down, frustrated, or confused—even about small things like pimples and weird voice cracks. He's never annoyed or too busy for you. You can give all of your worries to Jesus because he cares about you (1 Peter 5:7).

PUBERTY WON'T LAST FOREVER

Puberty feels long, but it's not forever. Your emotions will settle down. Your confidence will grow. You'll look back one day and realize how much God was doing in you through every awkward, confusing, and amazing part of the journey.

So when things feel tough, remember that God is growing you. With him you are strong, you are loved, and you are becoming exactly who God made you to be.

YOUR PUBERTY PERSONALITY

Growing up is a wild ride. So what kind of traveler are you on this puberty adventure? Answer these questions to find out!

Instructions: Keep track of your answers (A, B, C, or D), and check your results at the end!

1. When I think about my body growing taller and stronger, I feel . . .

A. Excited! I've been waiting for this.
B. Unsure. I have some questions.
C. Like I want to slow down. I'm not sure that I'm ready.
D. Like I want to skip to the part where it's done.

2. When my voice cracks or I get a pimple, I . . .

A. Laugh it off—it's part of the deal.
B. Want to know why it happens.
C. Hope nobody notices.
D. Feel super embarrassed.

3. When I see other boys growing faster than me, I . . .

A. Cheer them on—we're all in this!
B. Wonder when it'll be my turn.
C. Feel left out sometimes.
D. Compare myself and feel a little weird.

4. When I hear new info about puberty, I . . .

A. Think it's kind of cool!

B. Like learning how the body works.

C. Feel unsure and need time to think.

D. Want to pretend I didn't hear it.

5. When I have a question about puberty that feels awkward to ask, I . . .

A. Go for it—I'd rather ask than wonder.

B. Think carefully about who I should ask and what I want to know.

C. Wait a while until I feel more ready.

D. Keep it to myself and hope I figure it out somehow.

6. When my feelings get stronger or change fast, I . . .

A. Roll with it and keep going.

B. Try to figure out what's going on inside me.

C. Need a little space and time to settle down.

D. Feel confused or frustrated by myself.

7. When I remember that God made my body on purpose, I . . .

A. Feel confident—he's got me.

B. Feel safe—God doesn't make mistakes.

C. Want to believe it more.

D. Still feel a little awkward.

YOUR PUBERTY PERSONALITY RESULTS

MOSTLY A'S **The Adventurer**

You're charging into puberty like it's a new level in your favorite game. You're curious, brave, and ready to grow. Just remember that it's okay to slow down sometimes and ask questions when you need to.

MOSTLY B'S **The Explorer**

You like understanding what's going on. You want to figure out how your body works and why. Keep asking good questions and remembering that God made you with amazing detail and care.

MOSTLY C'S **The Slow-and-Steady Grower**

You're taking things one step at a time, and that's great. You might feel unsure about some changes, but you're still moving forward. God walks with you in every new experience, even the weird ones.

MOSTLY D'S **The Secret Agent**

You'd rather keep all these changes undercover. Puberty feels awkward, and you'd love to skip it. But guess what? God sees you, loves you, and is growing you in good ways, even when it's uncomfortable.

REGARDLESS OF YOUR "PUBERTY PERSONALITY," YOU ARE WONDERFULLY MADE BY GOD, AND EVERY PART OF YOUR GROWTH IS PART OF HIS GOOD PLAN. GOD IS WITH YOU, AND SO ARE THE PEOPLE WHO CARE ABOUT YOU.

4

GROWING —IN— WISDOM

GROWING ON THE INSIDE

Puberty isn't just about getting taller, growing muscles, or your voice cracking. It's also about who you're becoming on the inside. While your body is changing, you might start wondering, *What will I look like?* Or *Will I be like my friends?*

But a bigger, better question is who is God shaping me to be?

God cares about your body. He made it! But he also cares deeply about your character—your kindness, choices, and faith. As you grow stronger on the outside, God wants you to grow wiser and braver on the inside. Just like your muscles need food and exercise, your heart needs truth and wisdom to grow strong.

Growing in Strength, Courage, and Truth

As you get older, you'll start noticing more things—like how people treat each other, what's said in movies, and what friends post online. But not everything you hear or see lines up with God's truths. This is where wisdom kicks in.

Here's what the world might say:

- You have to be popular to matter.
- You need to look a certain way to be cool.
- You'll never be good enough.

Here's what God says:

- You are his. (Isaiah 43:1)
- He made you wonderfully. (Psalm 139:14)
- Nothing can separate you from his love. (Romans 8:38–39)
- You were created for a purpose. (Ephesians 2:10)

You get to decide which voice you'll listen to—the world's noise or God's truth. Real confidence doesn't come from having perfect hair or scoring the winning goal. It comes from knowing who you are in Christ.

Seeing the World Through God's Eyes

As your brain and heart grow, you'll start paying more attention to the things around you—like YouTube videos, video games, jokes, and what's popular on social media. You'll start noticing the world around you in new ways. You might see that friendships shift. You'll hear more about identity and success. Not all of it is bad, but not all of it is good either. Not everything you hear will match God's truths. That's why one of the most important parts of growing up is learning something called **discernment**, which means knowing the difference between what's *truly good* and what just *sounds good*. For example:

The world might say, "Your worth is in how athletic you are or how many people like you."	→	**But God says,** "You are valuable because you are mine, no matter what" (Isaiah 43:1).
Social media might say, "You need to change yourself to be accepted."	→	**But God says,** "You are my masterpiece, made on purpose" (Ephesians 2:10).
Your feelings might say, "You'll never be good enough."	→	**But God says** his love for you never depends on how perfect you are (Romans 8:38–39).

When people feel unsure about who they are, the world gives lots of different—and often confusing—answers about identity, beauty, strength, and worth. Here's something you can always hold on to: God has already spoken about who you are.

He made you on purpose and in his image (Genesis 1:27). Even when life feels confusing, you can trust that God's design is good. His love for you never changes. And when someone else is struggling with who they are, God calls you to respond with love (showing compassion) and truth (trusting his ways are good).

As you grow, you get to choose what voices you listen to. Ask God to help you trust what he says about you. When you know your identity is who God made you to be, not just how you look, you'll grow into someone full of confidence. Not because you have it all figured out, but because you trust the one who does.

GROWING IN LOVE AND WISDOM

Yes, puberty is a time of big changes. You'll grow taller, stronger, and maybe even hairier. But more importantly, God is growing your heart and faith. He's teaching you how to be kind when it's hard, how to stand strong in the truth, and how to be a young man who honors him. He is growing you in wisdom.

Wisdom uses technology cautiously. Social media, videos, and apps can seem fun, but they often make it look like you have to be a certain way to be liked. However, what you see online isn't always real. Filters change faces, and pictures are edited. Also, people usually share only their best moments, not their real, everyday struggles.

If you ever feel like you're not attractive enough, smart enough, or interesting enough, pause and ask yourself, *Am I believing what social media says about me, or what God says?* Instead of letting your phone shape how you see yourself, let God's truth be your guide. God says, "You are precious in my eyes, and honored, and I love you" (Isaiah 43:4 ESV).

Wisdom helps you guard what we see and think about. You might come across images, videos, or messages that aren't honoring to God—things that treat people like objects instead of creations made by him. If you see something that feels wrong, don't hide it. Talk to someone you trust. God never wants you to feel stuck in shame. He invites you to walk in truth and freedom (1 John 1:7).

Wisdom knows what to do with the thoughts that stick. You might feel tempted to think wrongly about yourself or others, or to look at something again, even when you know it isn't good. Temptation grows in the dark, but it shrinks when you bring it into the light. Sharing your temptations with someone you trust—like a parent, teacher, or church leader—helps break the power of shame. God's truth will also help you notice what's harmful, and when you ask for help, God will give you the strength to choose what's good.

Wisdom is learning to live God's way, even when you feel pulled in other directions. The more you open your heart to God and others, the stronger and freer you'll become. God's truth is a strong foundation that you can always stand on.

FRIENDS ARE GOD'S GIFT

Part of your growing includes learning how to treat others—your family, friends, and even girls—with care, respect, and kindness. As your body grows, so will your relationships. Let's talk about how to walk through those changes with wisdom and love.

God designed friendships as a beautiful gift! He made us to live in community—not alone—and to enjoy the love, laughter, and care that come with being close to others. In the Bible, we see amazing friendships, like David and Jonathan, who stuck together through hard times and helped each other follow God (1 Samuel 18). A good friend helps you do what's right, encourages you when you're down, and celebrates when things go well. Proverbs chapter seventeen says, "A friend loves at all times . . ." (v. 17). That means real friends don't just show up when things are fun. They stick with you even on the hard days.

God also wants us to be wise friends. That means treating others with kindness, respect, and truth and choosing friends who do the same for us. Proverbs teaches, "Walk with the wise and become wise, for a companion of fools suffers harm" (13:20). Friends shouldn't pressure us to do things that feel wrong or make us uncomfortable. That's not real friendship. Instead, a God-designed friendship helps you grow in love, joy, and courage.

Jesus even called us his friends (John 15:15), which means we can look to him as the perfect example of how to be loving, loyal, and full of grace. When we build friendships the way God intended, they become one of life's greatest joys.

Building Strong Friendships

Friendships and family relationships are a lot like building a tree house or a fort. Some are strong and steady, like a well-built tree house that can handle any storm. Others are more fragile, like something made out of sticks and tape that falls apart when things get tough. And sometimes, relationships feel more like a mess of broken boards and splinters. They hurt instead of help.

That's why we need wisdom when it comes to the people we're close to. God made us for relationships, but he also tells us to guard our hearts (Proverbs 4:23). That means being careful about who we let into our inner circle. We have to think about who we trust with our time, our thoughts, and our friendship. Some people are kind, loyal, and help us grow. Others may lie, tease, pressure us to do wrong, or treat us in hurtful ways.

Just like a builder puts up walls to keep the inside safe, you can set up limits. Limits are clear ways of saying, "This is how I expect to be treated," or "That's not okay." Limits don't mean being mean or pushing others away. They mean being wise about who helps you grow stronger in your faith, character, and courage—and who pulls you in the wrong direction.

What Makes a Good Friend?

A good friend helps you get closer to Jesus, not farther away. The Bible says, "Walk with the wise and become wise, for a companion of fools suffers harm" (Proverbs 13:20). In other words, the people you hang out with shape who you're becoming.

A true friend will

- encourage you to do the right thing—even when it's hard.
- have your back when you're having a rough day.
- tell the truth, even when it's not easy to hear.
- cheer for your wins instead of trying to compete with you.

Ask yourself, *Do my friendships bring me closer to God? Or do they pull me away?* Choosing good friends doesn't mean being unkind to others. It just means setting your anchor with the people who help you grow strong in your faith and love. And remember, Jesus was a friend to those who were hurting or left out. You can welcome and show kindness to everyone, even while choosing your closest friends wisely.

Speaking Life and Truth

Words are like seeds. They grow into something, whether good or bad.

The Bible says, "The tongue has the power of life and death..." (Proverbs 18:21). This means that our words can plant kindness and truth in the lives of our friends. Try saying words like these:

- You're great at including people."
- "That was awesome—you really worked hard."
- "You're so good at making people laugh."
- "You always know how to make someone feel like they belong."
- "God made you a one-of-a-kind person. That's seriously cool!"

The best friendships are the ones where both people are learning to be honest and kind. Be the type of friend who builds others up, like planting strong seeds that grow into something awesome. You can help goodness grow wherever you go.

Avoiding Words That Wound

Gossip is like mud on a clean jersey. It stains. Once it's there, it's hard to get off. While talking about someone behind their back might seem like no big deal, a rumor will spread fast and mess things up. The Bible says, "a gossip separates close friends" (Proverbs 16:28). Those cutting words land like a football tossed into a hornet's nest—suddenly everyone's running, and people get stung. God gave us words to build each other up, not to cause harm. James chapter three says that our words are powerful; like a tiny spark, they can start a wildfire (vv. 5–6).

If a buddy talks trash about other people to you, watch out! They'll probably talk the same way about you when you're not around. A real friend has your back, even when you're not in the room. God wants us to be the kind of friends who build each other up (1 Thessalonians 5:11). So if you hear gossip, you can walk away or say something like "Let's not talk about them like that." That's how strong, loyal friends act.

Handling Drama with Grace

Friendship drama can feel like a thunderstorm. It comes out of nowhere and shakes everything up. But just as storms pass, conflict doesn't have to ruin a friendship.

When arguments happen, don't turn to gossip or anger. Choose the path of peace (Romans 12:18). Try saying

- "I care about our friendship, and I want to understand what went wrong."
- "I'm sorry for my part in this. Can we work it out?"

Not every friendship will last forever, and that's okay. But even when things don't go the way you hoped, you can respond with grace, knowing that your worth isn't defined by what others think of you. Your worth is always defined by what God says about you.

Discovering Real Strength Isn't in Your Fists

Sometimes boys get into fights—at school, on the playground, or even with their own brothers. Maybe someone hurt your feelings, pushed you, or called you a name, and your instinct was to hit back. But God gives us a better way. His Word says, "Do not repay anyone evil for evil. Be careful to do what is right in the

eyes of everyone" (Romans 12:17). That means even when someone is mean or unfair, you don't have to fight back to prove your strength. Real strength is choosing self-control. Jesus taught us to love our enemies and to be peacemakers (Matthew 5:9). That doesn't mean letting people hurt you. It means asking for help, walking away when you can, and using your words instead of your fists.

If someone is hurting you or others, it's brave to speak up and get help from a trusted adult. Proverbs chapter fifteen says, "A gentle answer turns away wrath, but a harsh word stirs up anger" (v. 1). That's God's reminder that the way we respond can either stop a fight or start one. If you feel mad or out of control, take a pause and talk to God about it. He understands anger and wants to help you. Ephesians chapter six says, "Put on the full armor of God, so that you can take your stand against the devil's schemes" (v. 11). When you feel like fighting, ask Jesus to help you stand strong. Not with punches, but with patience, wisdom, and courage to do what's right.

Being the Friend Who Builds Others Up

Your words are powerful. That means what you say can either build people up or tear them down. You can encourage your friends by saying things like these:

- "I'm so glad you're here!"
- "You sure know how to have fun."
- "Thanks for being yourself."

Good friendships grow stronger when both people are kind, honest, and real. So don't wait—be the kind of friend you want to have.

Responding When Siblings Drive You Nuts (And How to Love Them Anyway)

Let's be honest: Siblings can be awesome—and annoying. One minute you're laughing together, and the next minute, they're teasing you. Sometimes it feels like they've turned into a totally different person overnight.

But here's what's really happening: They're growing up too. Just like your body and emotions are changing, so are theirs. That means they might be moodier, louder, more private, or just different than before.

God calls us to be peacemakers (Matthew 5:9), and that includes considering how we treat our brothers and sisters. That doesn't mean you won't argue (even best friends do!), but

it does mean choosing kindness—even when it's hard. Jesus gave us the Golden Rule: "So whatever you wish that others would do to you, do also to them . . ." (Matthew 7:12 ESV). So when a sibling frustrates you, take a deep breath and ask yourself, *How would I want to be treated right now?* Then ask God to help you act that way.

Relationships with siblings are some of the longest-lasting relationships you'll ever have. As with any strong team, it takes time, grace, and a lot of learning to work together well. But it's worth it.

GOD'S HELP AS WE GROW

This is a time of life when many things are changing all at once. Your body is growing, your emotions might feel strong, and your friendships might start to look a little different. It can feel exciting and confusing all at the same time! As you grow, you'll also start to notice more of the world around you. You'll have new experiences, learn new things, and have more opportunities to make choices on your own. This is a good thing because God designed us to grow and learn!

But not everything you come across will be good or helpful. Some things will be wonderful and honoring to God, like learning to be a kind friend, enjoying his creation, or discovering your talents. Other things aren't necessarily bad, but they might not help you love God or others well—like silly trends or games that don't really matter. Then there are things that tempt us to sin. You might feel pulled to lie, be mean to fit in, or choose what feels good instead of what is right. These moments are hard, but everyone faces them.

The good news is that we have a God who delights in helping us and forgiving us. He doesn't stand far away, waiting for us to figure it all out. He comes close to guide us and to pick us back up when we fall. So when you're not sure what to do, you can pray, "God, help me see what is good." And when you mess up, you can say, "God, I'm sorry. I need your forgiveness." And guess what? He loves to answer those prayers. He's the safest one to run to, no matter what.

We grow in love for God by depending on him each day. When we ask for help and forgiveness, we learn to trust him more. Each time we talk to him, we're drawing closer to his heart. As we walk with him, we discover how kind, strong, and faithful he is. Growing in love is not about being perfect, but about leaning on the one who is.

HEART CHECK

Have you ever stopped to notice what's happening not just in your body, but in your heart? Puberty brings big changes—new feelings, new thoughts, and new questions. Sometimes it can feel like a jumble, and that's okay.

Taking a little time to reflect is like holding up a mirror, not just to your face, but to your heart. When we pause and notice what we're feeling and wanting, we can bring it all to Jesus. He cares about every part of you.

The Bible says, "Keep your heart with all vigilance, for from it flow the springs of life" (Proverbs 4:23 ESV). That means what's going on inside of you really matters. Reflecting helps you spot the good things God is growing in you and also helps you see where you need his help and forgiveness.

So let's take a little "heart inventory." These questions aren't a test—they're a way to understand yourself better and invite God to walk with you as you grow:

- "What recent activity brought me excitement?"
- "What's worrying me?"
- "Who do I feel safest talking to when I'm upset?"
- "When do I feel most thankful?"
- "What do I usually do when I feel left out or ignored?"
- "What do I really, really want right now?"
- "When do I feel closest to God?"
- "Are there times that I pretend to be okay when I'm not?"
- "What do I hope other people think about me?"
- "What does God say about me that never changes, even when my feelings do?"

When you look inside your heart, you might see good things—like kindness, joy, or thankfulness. But you'll probably also see surprising things—like fear, jealousy, anger, or selfishness. That's true for every single person.

Here's the good news: Jesus came for hearts just like ours. He knows all about our sin, and he loves us anyway. He died on the cross to forgive us and rose again to give us new life. When we believe in him, we're not just left to figure things out on our own—Jesus gives us his Spirit to help us grow more like him every day.

So when you notice something hard in your heart, don't hide it. Bring it to Jesus. He forgives, he helps, and he promises never to let you go. That's what makes the gospel such good news!

HONORING YOUR PARENTS

Growing up can feel a little like standing on a seesaw. On one side, you want more freedom to stay up later, make your own choices, or do things your own way. On the other side, your parents are still guiding you, setting limits, and helping you grow. And that's actually a good thing! God gave them the role of teaching, protecting, and leading you in love (Deuteronomy 6:6–7).

Sometimes their rules might feel like a fence holding you in. But they're more like a trellis helping you grow. Think of a tall plant, like a tomato vine. It needs something sturdy to support it as it reaches upward. Without that support, it would bend, break, or grow in the wrong direction. Your parents' guidance is like that trellis. Their guidance is meant not to trap you, but to help you grow strong and steady.

As you get older, it's normal to want more independence. Wanting to grow up is part of how God designed you! But honoring your parents remains part of honoring God. That doesn't mean you'll always agree with them, but it does mean choosing respect in how you speak and act—even when it's hard. You might say things like these:

- "I'm trying to understand. Can we talk about it more?"
- "I hear what you're saying. Can I share my thoughts too?"

That's wisdom. Respect doesn't mean staying silent. It means growing stronger while still choosing to honor the people God placed in your life to help you. And as you mature, your respectful words and actions show that you're learning to follow Christ, even in the way you relate to your parents.

RESPECTING YOURSELF AND OTHERS

Your body and your space are a gift from God. It's kind of like having your own house. You get to decide who gets close and what behavior is allowed inside. Setting limits isn't mean; it's wise.

Here's what limits can look like:

- Saying no when someone pressures you to do something wrong or something you're not comfortable with.
- Speaking up if someone touches you or gets in your space in a way that feels wrong or uncomfortable.
- Taking a break from a friend who isn't treating you with respect.

Even Jesus wisely set limits! He rested when he needed to, told the truth with love, and walked away from people who were trying to hurt him. You're allowed to do the same.

Saying "No" Without Feeling Rude

Saying "no" can feel awkward. But it's okay to be clear and kind. Try saying statements like these:

A true friend will respect your "no." And if they don't, that's a red flag. Friendships should make you feel safe, not pressured.

TREATING PEOPLE WELL

Loving others doesn't mean always going along with everything others suggest. It means choosing kindness *and* honesty. Sometimes that means setting limits, saying "no," or even walking away from unhealthy friendships.

When you're not sure how to handle a situation, ask yourself, *Am I treating this person the way Jesus would want me to?*

Jesus stood up for what was right, spoke the truth, and loved people deeply—even when it was hard. You can do that too. It's okay to step back and not let some people into your inner circle. But even then, you're still called to treat them with respect because they're made in God's image, just like you. That means no mocking them, no gossiping about them, and no responding meanly in return. You can be kind and clear at the same time. God gives you wisdom to choose good friends and to treat everyone with love.

PEOPLE THAT GIVE YOU PAUSE

As you grow, you'll meet lots of different people. Some people will be kind and trustworthy, but others might show signs that they're not safe to be close to. Unsafe behavior can look like someone pressuring you to break rules, making fun of you or others, asking you to keep secrets, or wanting too much alone time with you in ways that feel uncomfortable.

Sometimes a person might act sweet in public but be sneaky or unkind in private. That can be really confusing! When you're unsure, don't try to figure it out all by yourself. God gives us wise parents, pastors, coaches, and teachers to help.

The book of Proverbs says, "in an abundance of counselors there is safety" (11:14 ESV). You can ask a trusted adult, "Does this seem okay to you?" or "What should I do if this person keeps acting like this?" Learning to tell the difference between safe and unsafe people takes time. God will help you grow wise and strong as you ask for help and walk in his truth.

Here are some things people do that should give you pause:

- They ask you to keep secrets from your parents or other adults.
- They touch you in a way that feels uncomfortable or confusing.
- They try to spend time alone with you and don't want others around.
- They make jokes or comments about your body.
- They pressure you to do things that feel wrong or scary.
- They try to give you gifts, money, or treats to keep you close.
- They don't respect your "no" or your personal space.
- They say things like, "Don't tell anyone about this."

If you notice any of these things, talk to a trusted adult right away. You're not being mean when you speak up. You're being wise and brave, just like God calls you to be.

Growing Stronger Together

God made you for friendship—not just to have fun, but to grow, encourage, and support one another. From the very beginning, he said it wasn't good for people to be alone (Genesis 2:18), and he designed relationships to be one of life's greatest gifts. Friends can help us laugh louder, stand taller, and feel braver. Some friendships come easily, like sunshine on a warm day. Others grow slowly, like seeds planted in good soil. But all healthy friendships need the same care: kindness, honesty, forgiveness, patience, and love.

Just like a campfire needs fuel and tending to stay bright, good friendships need time and attention. You build strong relationships by checking in, saying you are sorry, telling the truth gently, and choosing to stay—even when things get hard. Real friends celebrate with you, walk with you through messes, and help you become more like Jesus. Rather than tear you down, they build you up.

Being a faithful friend doesn't mean always agreeing or never struggling. It means showing up with love, wisdom, and grace. So ask yourself, *Am I being the kind of friend I hope to have? Do my friendships help me follow Jesus more closely?*

With God's help, you can build friendships that bring peace, joy, and strength. Be wise. Be kind. And trust him to help you grow into a friend who brings his light wherever you go.

USING TECHNOLOGY WISELY

As you grow up, your brain is learning how to focus, make decisions, and tell right from wrong. What you look at, listen to, and spend time on really matters—especially online. Phones, tablets, video games, and computers can be awesome tools. You can use them to learn new things, play games, make cool stuff, and stay connected.

But not everything online is good for your heart or your brain. Screens can pull you away from being the kind of person God is helping you to become. That's why your screen choices aren't just about rules. They're about honoring your growing heart and mind and using your time in ways that help you follow Jesus. They're about growing into the man God made you to be.

The Bible says, "Above all else, guard your heart, for everything you do flows from it" (Proverbs 4:23). That includes what you watch, listen to, post, and scroll through. Your heart is like the command center of your life. When you fill it with good things—truth, kindness, and creativity—you grow strong. But if you fill it with garbage, it starts to weigh you down.

SO, HOW CAN YOU USE SCREENS WISELY?

1. Let God's voice be louder than the internet's voice.

Have you ever felt like everyone online is shouting about what's cool, what's funny, or what you have to do to fit in? It's easy to think your worth comes from likes, followers, or others' attention.

But here's the truth:

- When the world says, "You're only important if you get attention," God says, "I have called you by name, you are mine" (Isaiah 43:1 ESV).
- When the world says, "Change yourself to be accepted," God says, "You are my masterpiece" (Ephesians 2:10, author paraphrase).

You don't need the internet to tell you who you are. You already belong to the God who made you.

2. Be a light, even online.

The Bible says, "The tongue has the power of life and death . . ." (Proverbs 18:21). That includes the words you text, type, or post. Before you hit send or comment, ask yourself, *Would I say this out loud in front of my parents or pastor? Is this building someone up or tearing them down?*

You can be someone who shares truth, spreads kindness, and walks away from drama—even in the digital world. That's what it means to follow Jesus while online.

3. Know when it's time to power down.

Screens aren't bad, but they can take over your time if you're not careful. Ever start playing a game or watching videos and realize that you've missed a whole afternoon? That's a sign that it's time to set some limits. Ask: *Is this helping me grow or wasting my time? Have I moved, talked with family, or spent time with God today?*

Think of your time like a backpack. If you fill it with too much screen time, there won't be room for the things that really matter—like prayer, friendship, rest, and real adventure.

And remember, the limits your parents set aren't meant to ruin your fun—they're there to protect you. God gives you parents to help you learn wisdom and self-control. When you respect the boundaries they set, you're not just obeying them—you're honoring God (Ephesians 6:1). If you don't understand a rule, talk about it. Ask questions kindly, and listen. Working together builds trust and shows maturity.

4. Stay safe and speak up.

The internet is a big place. Not everyone on it is safe or kind. Some people pretend to be someone they're not. Others might send messages, pictures, or videos that feel confusing, gross, or wrong. If that ever happens, you can stop, close the screen, and tell a trusted adult right away.

You are never in trouble for telling. In fact, telling is one of the bravest, strongest things you can do. God gave you a wise heart and a strong voice for a reason.

The Bible says, "The prudent see danger and take refuge . . ." (Proverbs 27:12). That means smart people don't stay in unsafe situations—they speak up and get help. So remember

- **Never share your name, address, or photos with someone online.**
- **Never keep secrets about things that make you feel weird or uncomfortable.**
- **If something feels wrong, you can say no, log off, and talk to a grown-up you trust.**

God cares about your heart, your body, and your safety. He wants you to live in the light and walk in his truth and promises.

Seeing Something You Shouldn't

Sometimes boys your age see pictures or videos online that show people without clothes or doing things meant for married couples—but in a twisted way that leaves out love, respect, and God's good design. These images might pop up by accident, or maybe a friend shows them to you. When that happens, you might feel surprised, curious, or even excited. That's a normal reaction—but those pictures don't show real love.

Looking at them is kind of like eating plastic fruit—it might look shiny and perfect, but it's not real, and it won't satisfy your hunger. In fact, it can make you sick. In the same way, those pictures take something beautiful that God made for marriage and twist it into something selfish and fake. **Over time, looking at them can hurt your heart—it can change the way you think about others and make it harder to see them the way God does.**

If that ever happens, **click away right away**—don't keep looking. Then talk to a parent, pastor, or another trusted adult. You're not in trouble. God wants to help you protect your heart and see others as special people made in his image—not as things to look at.

The Bible says, "Turn my eyes from looking at worthless things . . ." (Psalm 119:37 ESV).

Staying Grounded

Technology is pretty awesome. You can watch funny videos, play games, send messages, and learn new things in just a few taps. But sometimes all that screen time can start to feel like standing at a giant snack table. Some stuff is good for you, some looks cool but isn't really helpful, and some could even leave you feeling gross or distracted if you're not careful. And here's something important to know: A lot of apps and games are made to keep you coming back for more—kind of like candy that's designed to make you want another piece. That's

why it helps to be wise and set limit—so that screens don't end up bossing you around.

The internet, video games, YouTube, and social media aren't bad on their own. But how you use them matters. God calls us to be wise about what we consume, just like we are with the choices we make in other areas of everyday life. Whether you're texting a friend, watching videos, or choosing what game to play, ask yourself, *Is this helping me grow into the person God wants me to be?*

Noticing the Approval Trap: What Social Media Doesn't Tell You

Have you ever posted something or texted a friend and then kept checking to see who responded? Or watched a video and thought, *I don't look like that guy*, or *Why is his life cooler than mine?* That's something almost everyone feels sometimes, but it's a trap.

Social media makes it easy to think that likes, views, or followers decide how valuable you are. Consider these contrasts:

When the world says, "You're only important if people notice you," →	**God says,** "I have called you by name, you are mine" (Isaiah 43:1 ESV).
When the world says, "You have to be perfect to be liked," →	**God says,** "Nothing can separate you from his love" (Romans 8:38–39).

You don't need the internet to tell you who you are. The God who created you already approves of you. That's way better than a million likes.

Being Wise Online

Think of your mind like a Minecraft world. You're always building something. If you fill it with truth, kindness, and good stuff, it gets strong. But if you let in junk—like mean comments, gross videos, or bad language—it starts to break down your world from the inside.

Before you watch, play, post, or comment, try asking yourself these questions:

- *Would I say this out loud in front of my parents?*
- *Is this helping me follow God or pulling me away?*
- *Would I feel proud or ashamed if someone saw this?*

Setting limits online isn't about being afraid or "missing out." It's about protecting what matters most. And that is your heart, your mind, and your time with God.

The Bible says, "The prudent see danger and take refuge . . ." (Proverbs 27:12). That means wise people step away from things that might be harmful. God wants you to use the internet in a way that protects your heart, your mind, and your body. When in doubt, choose safety. You are precious to God. He delights in helping you stay safe and strong.

Making Time for What Really Matters

Have you ever started watching videos and suddenly realized an hour has gone by? Or spent so much time on your phone that you didn't even notice the people around you? Here's a challenge:

- Instead of grabbing your device first thing in the morning, read a Bible verse or pray.
- Instead of scrolling when you're bored, go outside, build something, draw, or spend face-to-face time with a friend.

Take a break from your screen each day, and notice how you feel. Use technology with wisdom. Set limits. Stay rooted in what's real. And remember: You already belong, already have worth, and are already loved. No screen can give you that, and no screen can take it away.

Bottom line: You're in charge. Technology is a gift, but it should never be your boss. Use it with purpose. Let God shape what you see, say, and do online. You were made for something way more powerful than a screen. You were made to follow Jesus and bring his light wherever you go—even into the digital world.

WHO'S IN CHARGE: YOU OR YOUR SCREEN?

Wondering how your screen habits are shaping your days? **Try this quiz to find out!**

1. What's the first thing you do when you wake up?

A. Grab my tablet or game controller right away.

B. Get ready, eat breakfast, then check my device.

C. Talk to God, stretch, or start my day with no screen in sight.

2. How often do you take breaks from screens?

A. Breaks? What breaks? I usually get sucked in.

B. Sometimes, but I'm not really paying attention to it.

C. I take screen breaks and do other fun stuff, like going outside or creating something.

3. What do you do before bedtime?

A. Watch videos or play games until I can't keep my eyes open.

B. Use my device for a bit, but try to stop in time for a good night's sleep.

C. Read, pray, or talk with my family—no screens allowed at bedtime!

4. How do you feel after lots of screen time?

A. Kinda grumpy, tired, or just blah.

B. Meh—it's okay, but I sometimes wish I'd done something else.

C. Pretty good, because I keep things balanced.

5. Your friend asks you to come play outside, but you're halfway through a video. What do you do?

A. Say, "No thanks," and keep watching.

B. Tell them you'll come out after the video ends.

C. Pause the video and head outside—real fun > screen fun.

YOUR SCREEN TIME RESULTS

MOSTLY A'S Screen Overload Zone

Uh-oh! It looks like screens are taking up a lot of your time—and maybe your energy too. Don't worry though! You can start setting limits and try something new, like riding your bike, reading a cool book, or hanging out with friends. Your brain (and your heart) will thank you.

MOSTLY B'S Almost Balanced

You're on your way! You're thinking about screen time, but you still have some work to do. Try building a screen routine—add in some reading, prayer, movement, and face-to-face fun to keep things healthy and strong.

MOSTLY C'S Screen Time Pro

Nice work! You're using screens in smart ways and making space for what really matters—friends, faith, fun, and family. Keep being wise and setting the example for others too.

Creating a Healthy Screen-Time Routine

- **Set limits**—Decide how much time you'll spend on screens each day.
- **Take breaks**—Move around, read, or play outside between screen sessions.
- **No screens before bed**—Give your brain time to rest!
- **Choose wisely**—Pick activities that help you grow, not just waste time.
- **Stay connected**—Spend time with family and friends offline too!

And remember, God gives you parents to help you learn wisdom and self-control. If you ask them for help, they might have some great tips for your healthy screen-time routine. They have to navigate their own screen time, too.

Protecting Your Digital Integrity: Following Jesus Online

What if everything you said and did online popped up on a giant screen in the middle of your school? Would you still say it? Would you make the same posts? The Bible says, "The tongue has the power of life and death . . ." (Proverbs 18:21), and that applies to what we type just as much as what we say.

Here are some tips for keeping your online life strong and honest:

- Remember that words can build up or tear down. Before posting or commenting, ask yourself, *Would I say this to someone's face?* If not, don't type it.
- Skip the drama. If a group chat turns into gossip or name-calling, you can be the one who steps back or speaks up.
- Remember that you represent Christ. Even online, your actions show others who you follow. Be kind, honest, and wise.

And hey—if you mess up (we all do sometimes), don't try to hide it. Maybe you said something unkind or watched something you know you shouldn't have. Tell God you're sorry, talk to a trusted adult, and ask for wisdom to move forward. The internet is full of temptations, but you can choose to be a light.

Guarding Your Heart Online

Not everything online is good for you. Some things aren't true, some things can hurt your heart, and some things just fill your mind with stuff that doesn't help you grow. That's why having rules isn't a bad thing. They're actually good! God gives us boundaries to keep us safe and free. It's kind of like a fence around a playground. Fences do not take away your fun; they help you have fun while staying safe.

Good digital limits might include:

- Choosing to put away devices during family time or before bed so that your mind can rest.
- Deciding not to follow people who make you feel insecure or envious.
- Saying "no" to messages, images, or videos that make you feel uncomfortable or unsure.

And if you ever see or experience something online that doesn't feel right, tell a trusted adult. God didn't design us to figure things out by ourselves. He gave us parents, teachers, and mentors to help us walk in wisdom and truth.

Being a Light

The internet is full of noise. But you don't have to follow the crowd. You can shine like a light by being kind, truthful, and wise—even online. Whether you're playing games, chatting with friends, or just scrolling, remember that you are God's precious child. You represent him to others. Because you belong to God, your choices, and even your clicks, can honor him.

REMEMBER WHO YOU ARE

It's totally normal to want to be noticed. Maybe you want your friends to laugh at your joke, your dad to say, "Nice shot," or your coach to see you hustle. That's not weird; it's part of how God made us. We like to be seen, known, and cheered on.

But sometimes we start thinking that the only way to feel good is by other people noticing us. We chase likes, compliments, or attention. That's when we need to stop and remember that our worth doesn't come from how many people see us. It comes from the one who made us.

God says, ". . . I will not forget you! See, I have engraved you on the palms of my hands . . ." (Isaiah 49:15–16). That means God never loses sight of you. He knows your name. He sees your heart. His love is locked in. It never changes, even when you feel off, awkward, or unsure.

People's opinions can flip-flop like a fish on a dock. But God's love? Rock solid. Always steady. Always true. So next time you're online and think:

Do I look cool enough?
Why didn't anyone like that?
Am I good enough?

Remember this: You are already more than "liked." You are loved by the God of the universe. That's way better than a million likes!

There are lots of voices online. Voices telling you who to be, what to wear, and how to act. But the most important voice is God's. Here's what *he* says about you:

- You are loved. (Romans 8:38–39)
- You are wonderfully made. (Psalm 139:14)
- You were made to shine for him. (Matthew 5:16)

So don't let your screen tell you who you are. Let God's truth shape you. He made you to shine and bless others, not to impress them. Use your words to encourage others, post things that build people up, and be wise and kind online.

Screens need a strong heart behind them. And with God's help, you've got one.

CONCLUSION: BECOMING THE MAN GOD MADE YOU TO BE

Puberty isn't just something to "get through." It's part of how God is preparing you for the future. Every change—getting stronger, thinking more deeply, feeling new emotions—is shaping you into the young man God designed you to be. Your body isn't growing for no reason. God is getting you ready to love him and love others wherever he calls you—maybe as a firefighter, teacher, coach, missionary, neighbor, or a dad.

Growing Up Like Jesus

Getting older isn't only about gaining height and a deeper voice—it's about your heart and character. The Bible says, "Jesus grew in wisdom and stature, and in favor with God and man" (Luke 2:52). He didn't just grow taller; he grew in wisdom, kindness, and obedience to God. You can grow that way too—you stretch each time you tell the truth, help someone, forgive, or trust God when life feels confusing.

Remembering the Good News That Grounds You

Before you were born, God knew your name and loved you (Jeremiah 1:5). He made you on purpose—with your smile, your laugh, your body, and your heart.

But sin separates us from God, so we need a rescuer. That's why Jesus came. He lived perfectly, died to take away our sin, and rose again so that we can belong to God forever. When you trust in Jesus, you are

- fully forgiven,
- a child of God,

- filled with his Spirit,
- being made new every day, and
- loved forever—no matter what.

Your worth isn't in how you look, how fast you grow, or how well you do in school. Your worth is found in the one who made you and gave his life for you. He says you are his and you are loved.

Considering This as a Time of Becoming

Instead of thinking, *I just want to get puberty over with*, try thinking, *God is shaping me for something important.* Even the awkward or hard parts can make you stronger, kinder, and wiser.

God's plan for you stays the same. **Your purpose is to**

- glorify God,
- love people well, and
- grow into the young man he made you to be.

Pocketing Truths for Tough Days

- **Your confidence rests in Christ:** Your value is rooted in Jesus, not in size, speed, grades, or opinions.
- **You're not alone:** God is with you, and he gives you parents, friends, and mentors to walk beside you.
- **This season won't last forever:** Bodies and feelings find their rhythm. You'll look back and see how God was growing you.

Bottom line: Even as you change, one thing never changes—God's love for you. Because of Jesus, you are forgiven, treasured, and made new. Your identity isn't shifting like your body—it's secure in Christ. You belong to him. You are God's beloved son, now and forever.

Growth Goals

Growing up is more than just physical changes—it's about your heart, mind, and faith growing too! Jesus grew in wisdom, strength, and favor with God and others (Luke 2:52). Let's think about how you're growing and set some goals for the kind of young man you want to become.

1. Physical Growth

Your body is changing—God is helping you grow strong and healthy.

GOAL: One way I can take care of my body this week is:

2. Wisdom & Choices

Wisdom means knowing what's right and choosing to do it—even when it's hard.

GOAL: One wise choice I want to make this week is:

3. Emotional Growth

God gave you feelings, and he can help you handle them well.

GOAL: When I feel frustrated or overwhelmed, I want to:

4. Spiritual Growth

Jesus grew closer to God. You can too!

GOAL: One way I want to grow in my faith this week is:

5. Relationships

God calls us to treat others with kindness and love.

GOAL: One way I can show love to a friend or family member is:

BONUS VERSE TO REMEMBER:

"Jesus grew in wisdom and stature, and in favor with God and man." (Luke 2:52)

APPENDIX: A NOTE TO PARENTS AND CAREGIVERS

Parents, your son is stepping into an important season of growth. He might feel excited, uncertain, or even nervous about what's ahead. He needs your wisdom, patience, and reassurance. The best way to walk through this with him is to create a safe, open space where he knows he can ask questions and be heard.

This book is designed to help you start important conversations with your son about his changing body and emotions, all while keeping God's truth at the center. We encourage you to read through these chapters together, answer his questions with honesty and gentleness, and remind him often that he is deeply loved by God—and by you.

Walking with Him Through Every Change

Puberty is more than a phase—it's a God-designed season of growth that includes the body and the heart. As your son enters this unfamiliar territory, he needs more than facts. He needs your presence, wisdom, and steady assurance that he is not alone.

Think of this book as a tool in your hands—it offers words, examples, and conversation starters, but you know your child best. Follow his questions, notice where he is wrestling, and let the material be a springboard for deeper heart conversations. You can make direct applications to where you see his heart is struggling and take the material deeper, but you don't have to do it all at once. For example, if you notice he often gets discouraged or angry when things don't go his way, you could pause and talk about how our emotions can sometimes lead us to sin—like snapping at others or giving up hope. Then you can remind him that Jesus cares about his feelings, forgives him when he sins, and gives him strength to respond with patience and trust instead.

Below you'll find conversation starters, help for answering awkward questions, and a note of encouragement for both dads and moms.

Conversation Starters

Boys often don't come with a lot of words, but that doesn't mean they don't have questions. Here are some open-ended starters to gently begin the conversation:

- "Was there anything in this chapter that seemed weird, cool, or surprising?"
- "Is anything about growing up feeling confusing or hard for you?"
- "I know these changes can be awkward to talk about—but I'm always here for real conversations."
- "When I was your age, I wondered about ___. Do you ever think about that?"
- "Do you want to talk about anything from what you've read, or should I just check in from time to time?"

Sometimes conversations go best during shared activities like driving, walking, or working side by side on something.

What to Do When It Gets Awkward

Awkward questions are normal—and they're not a sign that something's gone wrong. Here's what you can do:

- **Don't panic.** A calm, "That's a good question—let's talk about it," helps him know you're safe and not shocked.
- **Don't rush.** Let him process in pieces. He might come back later with more thoughts.
- **Be honest.** If you don't know something, say so. The statement "Let's look into it together" builds trust.

- **Keep the big picture in view.** Whether he's asking about wet dreams, shaving, or private parts, remind him often that every part of his body, emotions, and questions are part of God's good design.

Your comfort will become his compass. If you treat topics like erections, voice cracks, or awkward emotions as normal and navigable, he will too.

A Note for Parents of Boys with Disabilities

Puberty can feel extra complicated when your son lives with a disability or medical condition. But here's the good news: His worth is not measured by what his body can or cannot do. He is fearfully and wonderfully made (Psalm 139:14), and every part of him is wrapped in God's good design. Jesus had a special love for people with difficult conditions.

Here are some truths to keep pointing him to and ways to talk about them:

1. GOD'S IMAGE IS NOT DIMINISHED.

What to say: "You reflect God's image fully—not partly. He made you to show his beauty and love in ways that only you can."

Why it matters: Children with disabilities sometimes feel "less than." Root his identity in Christ, not in abilities.

2. WEAKNESS SHOWS GOD'S STRENGTH.

What to say: "When things feel hard, God's strength shines through you. He loves to use your life to show his power and grace" (see 2 Corinthians 12:9–10).

Why it matters: Disability is not wasted—it can become a platform for experiencing God's help.

3. YOU ARE MORE THAN WHAT YOU CAN DO.
What to say: "Your worth isn't in how fast you run, how clearly you speak, or how much you can do. Your worth is in belonging to Jesus, and that never changes."
Why it matters: The world often defines kids by their abilities. God defines them by his love.

4. THE CHURCH NEEDS YOU.
What to say: "God made you an important part of his family. Every person in God's family has an important and special role to play" (see 1 Corinthians 12:22–23).
Why it matters: Children with disabilities may feel like outsiders. Show him he is needed and honored in the body of Christ.

5. WE ALL HAVE THE HOPE OF HEAVEN.
What to say: "One day, Jesus will give you a brand-new body that will never hurt or grow tired. But even now, he is with you and delights in you" (see Revelation 21:4).
Why it matters: It offers him both present comfort and future hope.

A Word for Dads (and Moms Too)

As your son grows, he's watching you. Not just your answers, but your attitude toward your own body, your responsibilities, and your faith.

That includes how he views his body. Boys notice strength—yours and theirs. Whether you're lean, muscular, or somewhere in between, your attitude toward your own body sends a message. When you thank God for your body instead of criticizing it, when you show him that strength isn't just about muscles but about character and courage, you're training his heart. Help him see his body not just as something to look at, but as something to use—to love God and care for people. Guide him to see using his body as part of worship: All he has—big or small—can be offered to love God and neighbor.

If you're a mom, you might feel unsure how to guide him through body changes you've never experienced yourself. That's okay. Your gentleness, respect for his growing independence, and faith-filled encouragement are still vital. You don't need to explain every detail—you just need to stay connected.

And if you're parenting alone or navigating tricky dynamics, take heart: God promises to give wisdom generously (James 1:5) and to be a Father to the fatherless (Psalm 68:5). He is with you and your son every step of the way.

FINAL ENCOURAGEMENT

You don't need all the right words. You just need to keep showing up. Your son is not looking for a perfect parent—he's looking for someone who listens, laughs, guides, and gently tells him the truth about who he is.

Keep pointing him back to the God who made his body good, who sent Jesus to redeem it, and who will one day make all things new.

You're not just helping him grow up—you're helping him grow strong in grace.